Topsy and Tim's New Brother

Jean and Gareth Adamson

Blackie: Glasgow and London

Copyright © 1975 Jean and Gareth Adamson

ISBN 0 216 90104 9 (Paperback)
ISBN 0 216 90105 7 (Hardback)

Blackie and Son Limited
Bishopbriggs, Glasgow G64 2NZ
5 Fitzhardinge Street, London W1H 0DL

Printed in Great Britain by
Butler & Tanner Limited
Frome and London

Everyone was busy at Topsy's and Tim's house, preparing for a new baby. Tim and Dad got Tansy's old cot down from the loft.

When Mummy agreed it was clean in all the corners they painted it to match the new chest of drawers.

Tim stuck the decorations on.
"Doesn't that look super!" said Tim.
"You've got paint on your nose,"
Topsy told him.

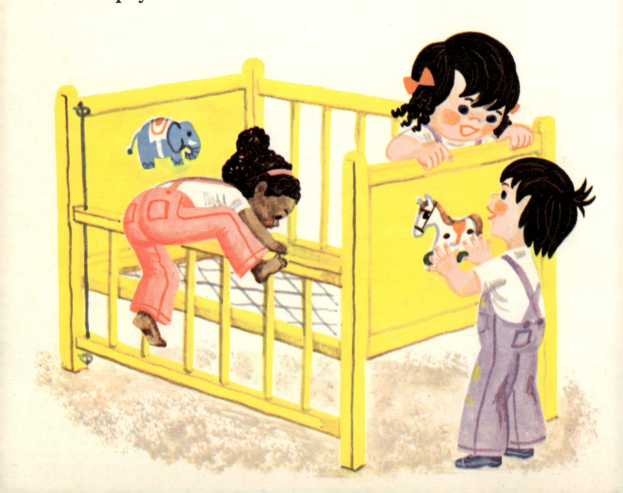

Topsy and Mummy got the baby's clothes ready. Some were new. Some had once been Topsy's or Tim's. None really needed washing, but Topsy and Mummy washed them just the same.

"You've got bubbles on your nose," Tim told Topsy.

Tansy polished the pram and made sure it worked well. Mummy bought a safety net to stop Kitty from sitting on the baby.

Topsy and Tim told their teacher, Miss Maypole, "We're going to have a baby brother."
"We are adopting him, like we adopted Tansy," said Topsy, "because he has lost his own Mummy and Dad and needs a new family."
Miss Maypole told the class this exciting news.

Mrs Tippitt came to tea.

It was Mrs Tippitt's job to make sure that the baby would have a good home.

"Some of these clothes used to be mine," said Topsy.

Mrs Tippitt thought Topsy's and Tim's was a very good home.

"What will you call your new brother?" she asked.

"Flash," said Tim.

"We're not going to wash the floor with him!" said Topsy. "Anyway, all our names start with T."

"Call him 'P. G. Tips' then," said Tim. "That's tea."

"Teddy would be a nice name," said Topsy.
"Ugh!" said Tim, but Mrs Tippitt said, "Teddy is short for Théodore, and that means 'a gift from God'. I think that would be a lovely name for him."

Dad took them to the Adoption Centre to meet baby Teddy. Everyone was excited except Tim. "Why do we need another boy?" said Tim.

Mummy and Dad had to sign a lot of papers. "Come and see Teddy while we are waiting," said Mrs Tippitt.

Baby Teddy was darker than Topsy and Tim, but not so dark as Tansy. He would not let go of Tim's finger.

Mrs Tippitt let Topsy and Tim carry him – very carefully – to meet his new Mummy and Dad.

Tansy and Mummy were to take Teddy
to the Health Centre next morning
while Topsy and Tim were at school.
"I want to go with Teddy," said Tim.
He did, too, very much.

The telephone rang. It was Miss Maypole.

She wondered if Topsy and Tim would like a special holiday as it was Teddy's first day at home.

"Where's Tansy?" said Mummy.
Tansy had gone to tell her friend
Dr Jaunty about her new baby brother.
She brought her to meet Teddy.

When they got home, Tim helped Mummy prepare Teddy's milk. The printing on the box told how much powder to use. Tim measured it very carefully.

They did not want Teddy to be too fat or too thin.

Teddy was ready for his bottle.

Next morning, very early, Topsy and Tim and Tansy tiptoed in to peep at Teddy.

"Can we take him to school?" asked Topsy and Tim.

"What an idea!" said Dad. "He's not a toy."

When schooltime came, Teddy was ready for a pram-ride.

"We can go with Topsy and Tim," said Tansy.

Topsy's and Tim's school friends ran to meet Teddy. Miss Maypole said she had never seen a nicer baby.

Topsy and Tim and Tansy felt very proud of their new baby brother.